Jesus Is Alive

The text of these books has been rewritten on the basis of Today's English Version to keep as much of the New Testament stories as can be understood by the intended readers.

Illustrations by de Kort

First United States Paperback Edition 1977

Original Dutch Version copyright © 1968
Netherlands Bible Society, Hilversum

English Text copyright © 1975
British and Foreign Bible Society

International Standard Book No. 0-8066-1579-6

Manufactured in the United States of America

P242

AUGSBURG PUBLISHING HOUSE
MINNEAPOLIS, MINNESOTA

EMORY UNITED METHODIST CHURCH

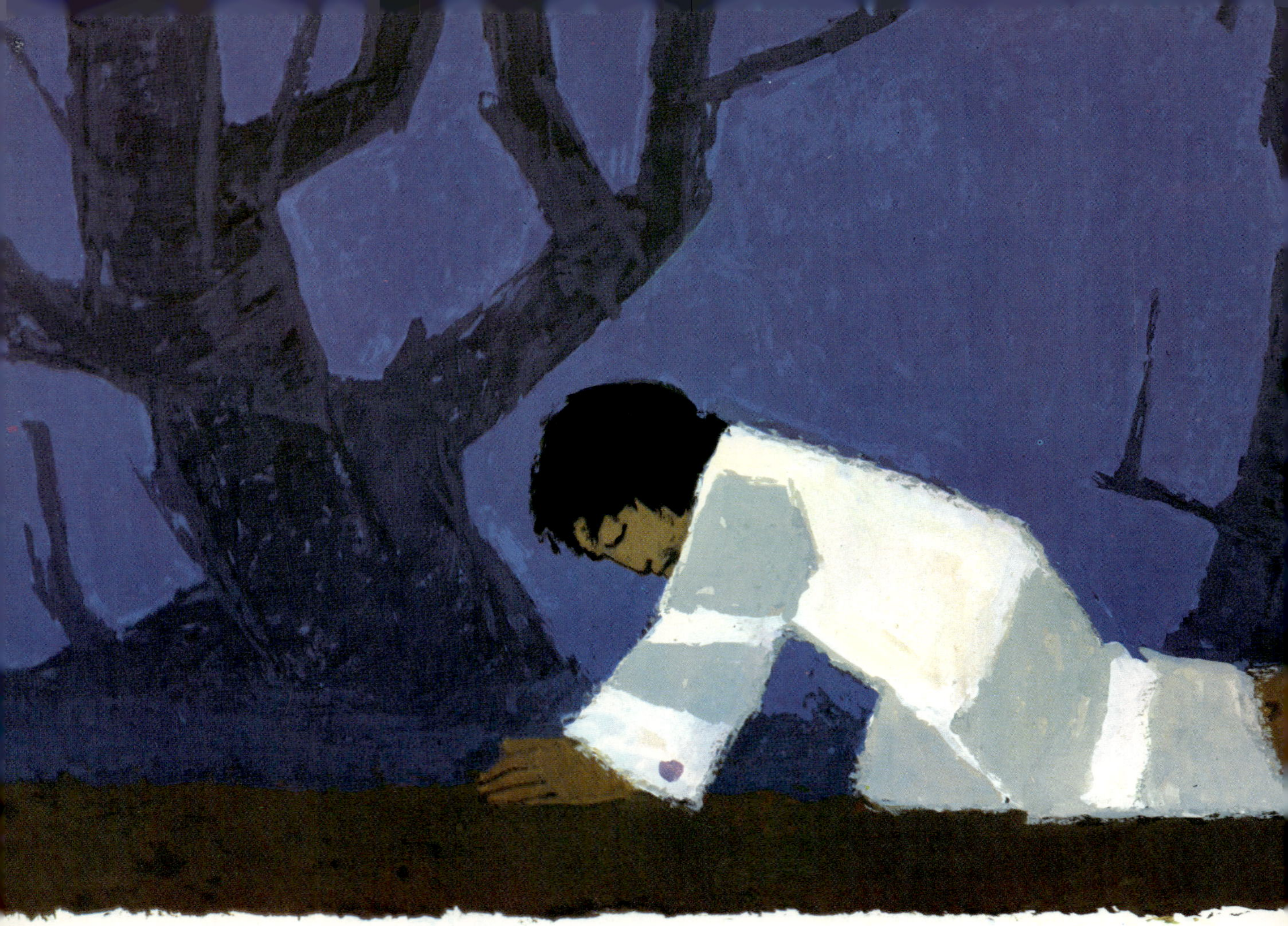

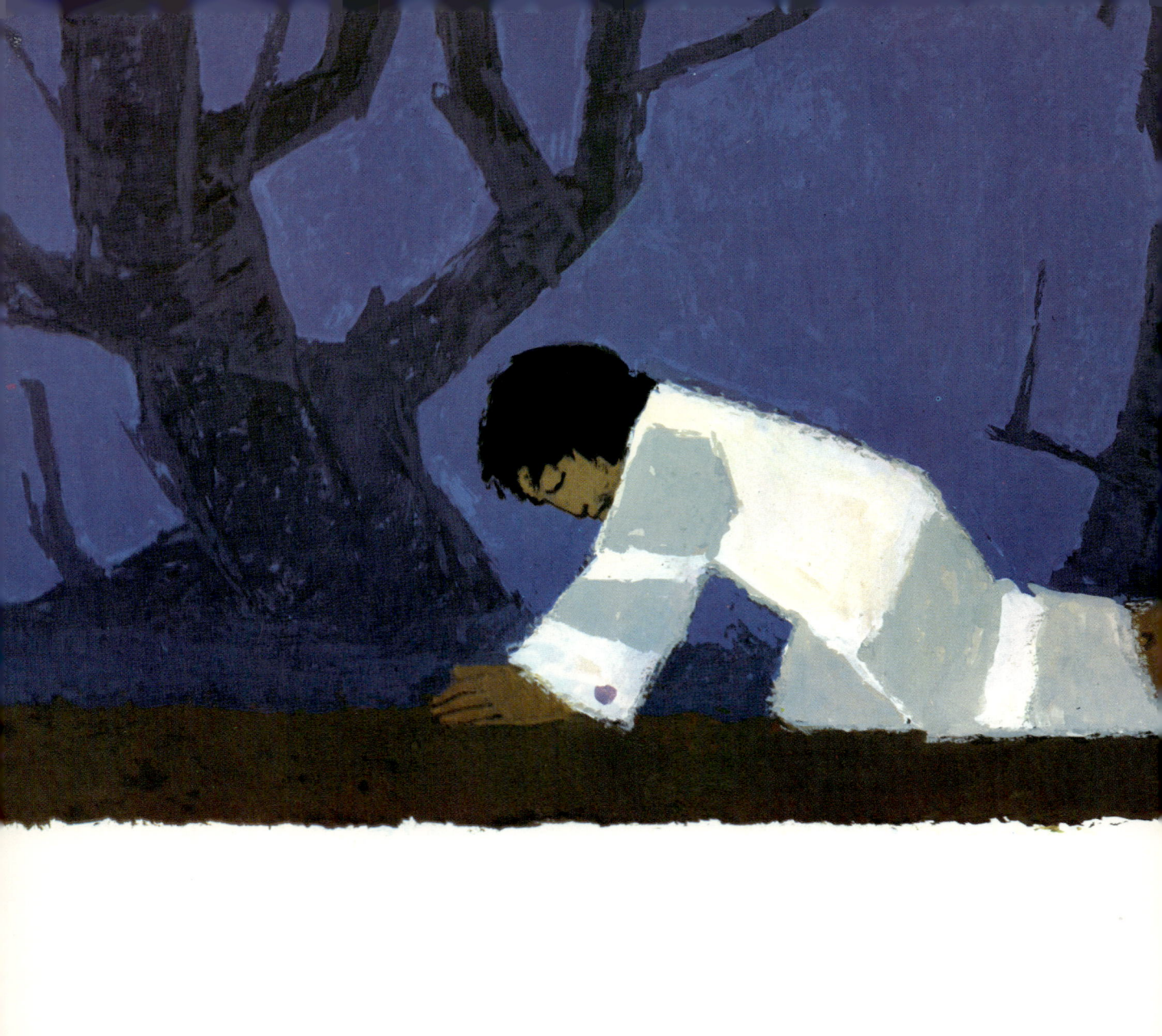

Jesus went with his friends to a garden.
He prayed, "My Father, do what you want to me."

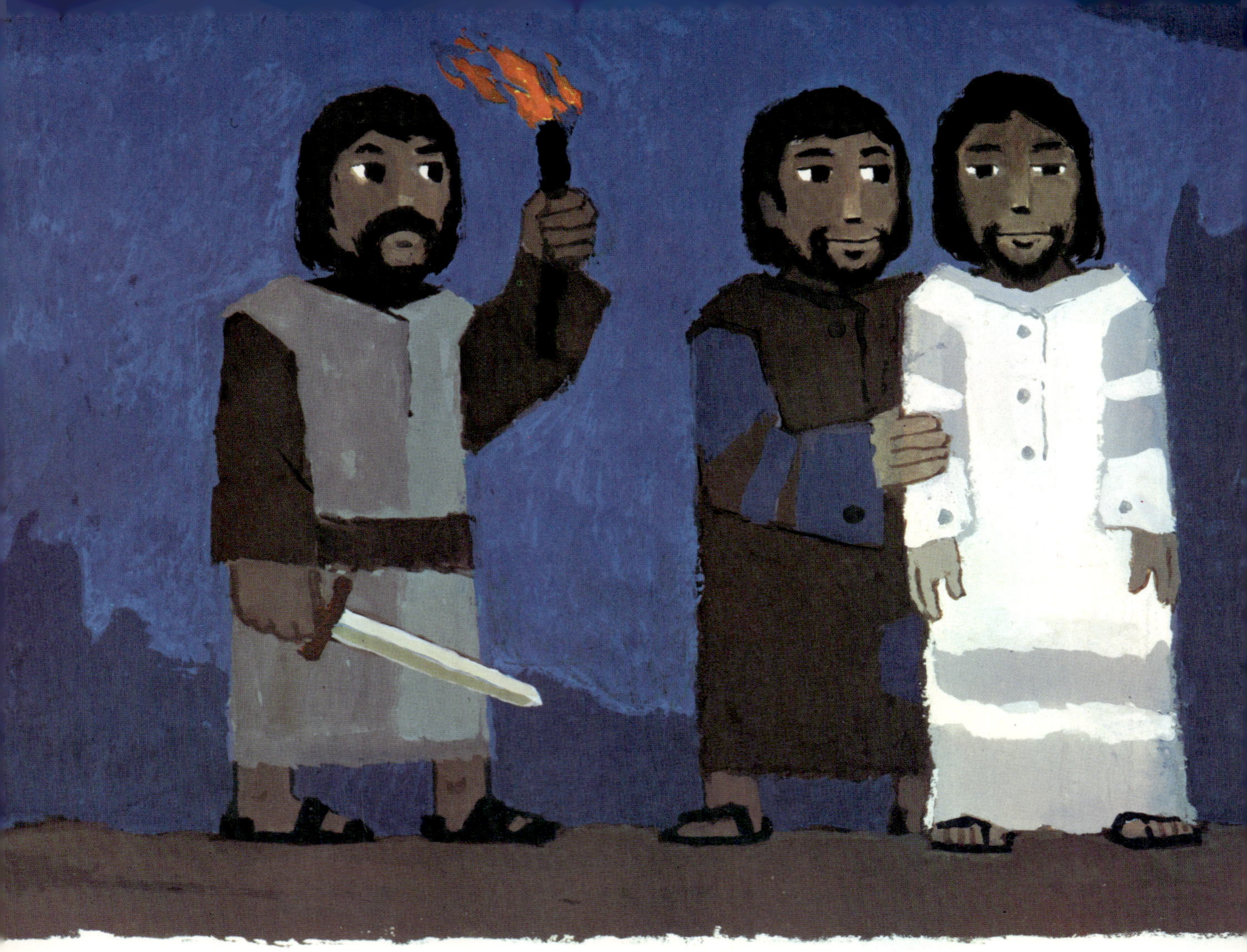

Then Judas came with some soldiers.
They took Jesus away.

The soldiers took Jesus to the chief priest.
The chief priest asked Jesus, "Are you God's son?"
Jesus said, "I am."

The chief priest and the other judges said,
"He says he is God's son.
He is a liar! He must die!"

They took Jesus to Pilate.
The soldiers dressed him like a king.
They put a red robe on him
and a crown of thorns on his head.

Then they made fun of him.
Pilate said, "Put him on a cross to die."

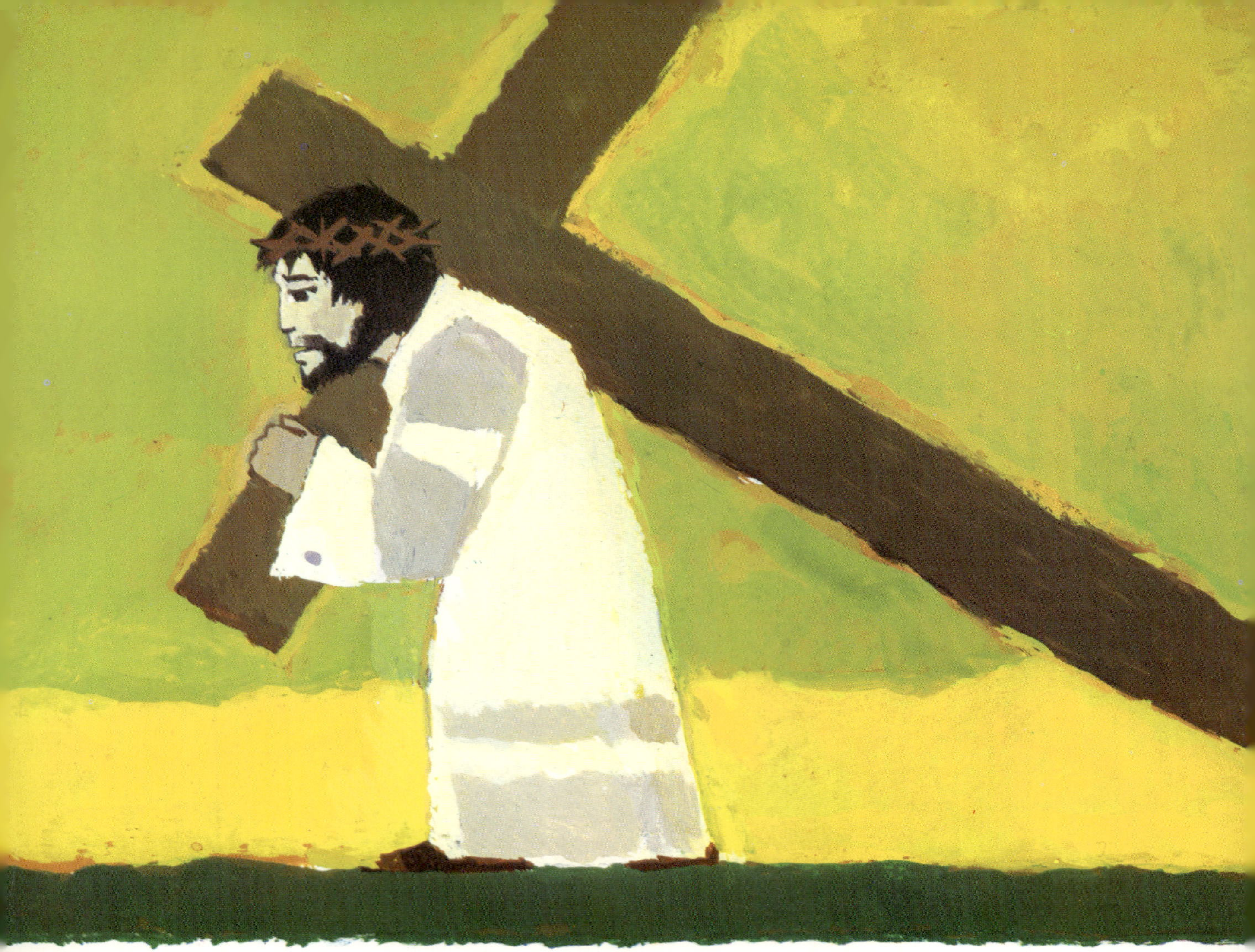

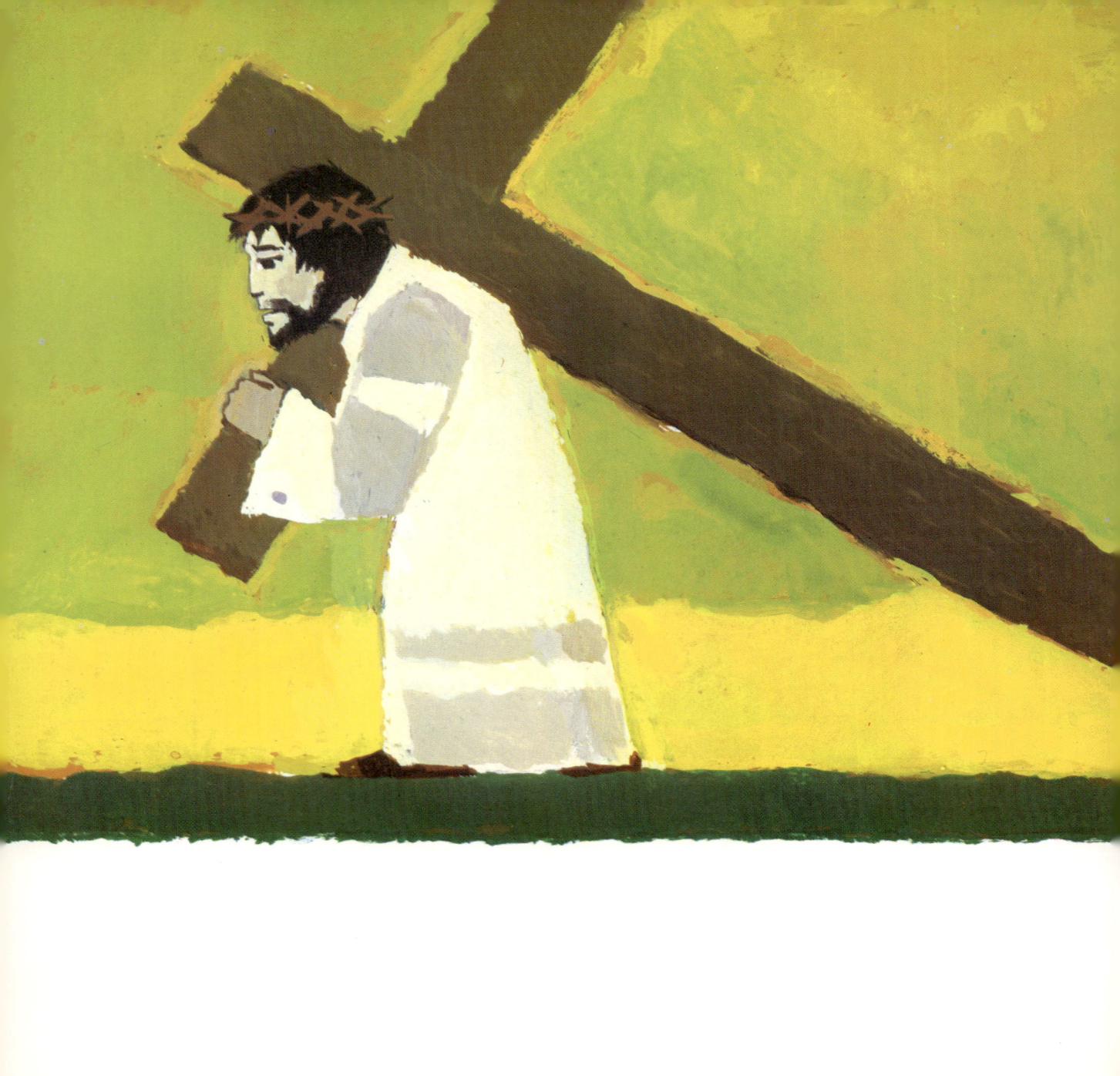

The soldiers took Jesus to a hill near the town.
The hill was called Calvary.

Jesus was put on the cross.
Jesus' mother was called Mary.
Mary stood nearby with Jesus' friend, John.
Jesus said to them,
"John, be like a son to my mother.
Mother, look after John."

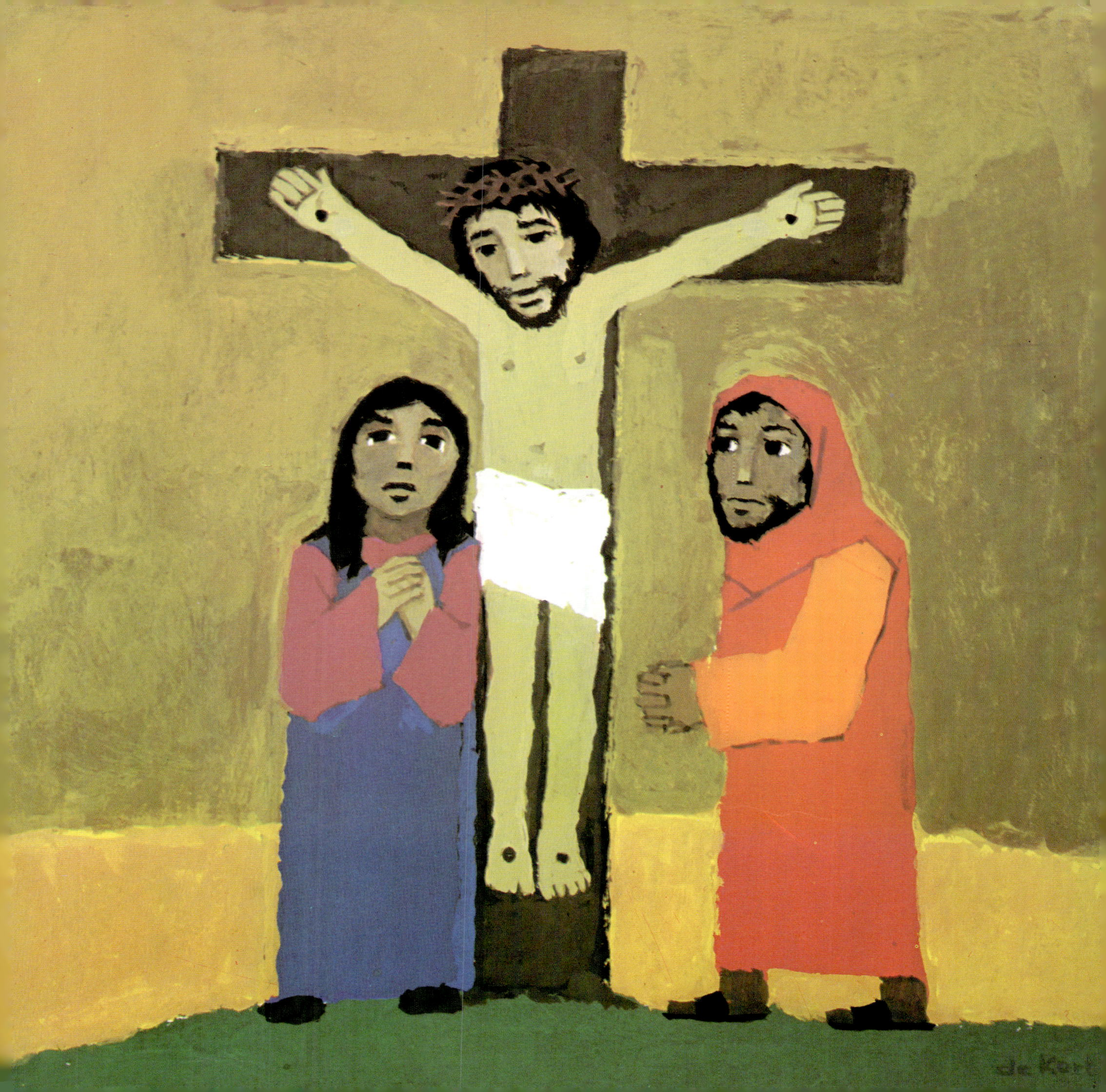
de Kort

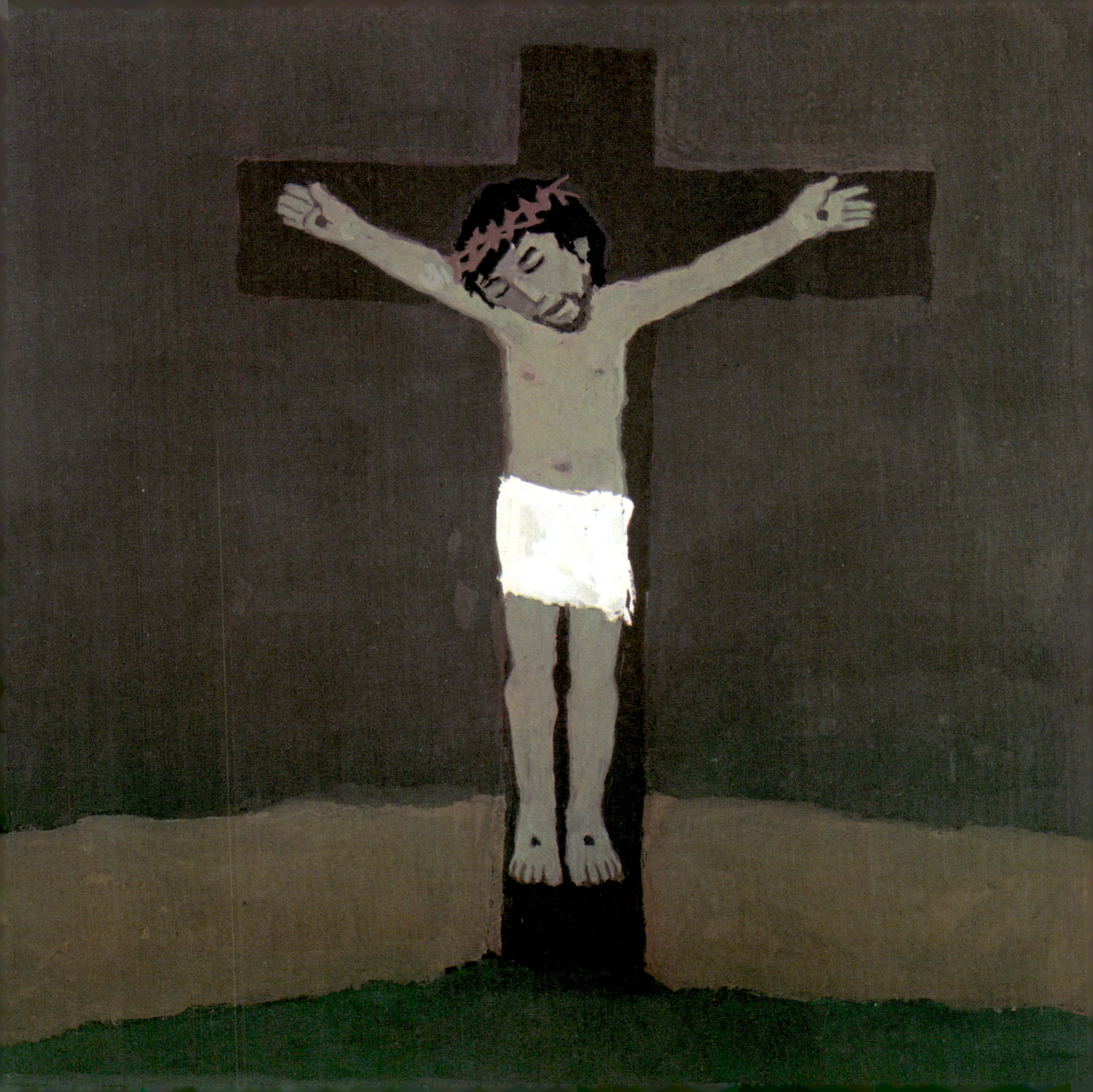

Then Jesus said, "It is done."
He bowed his head and died.

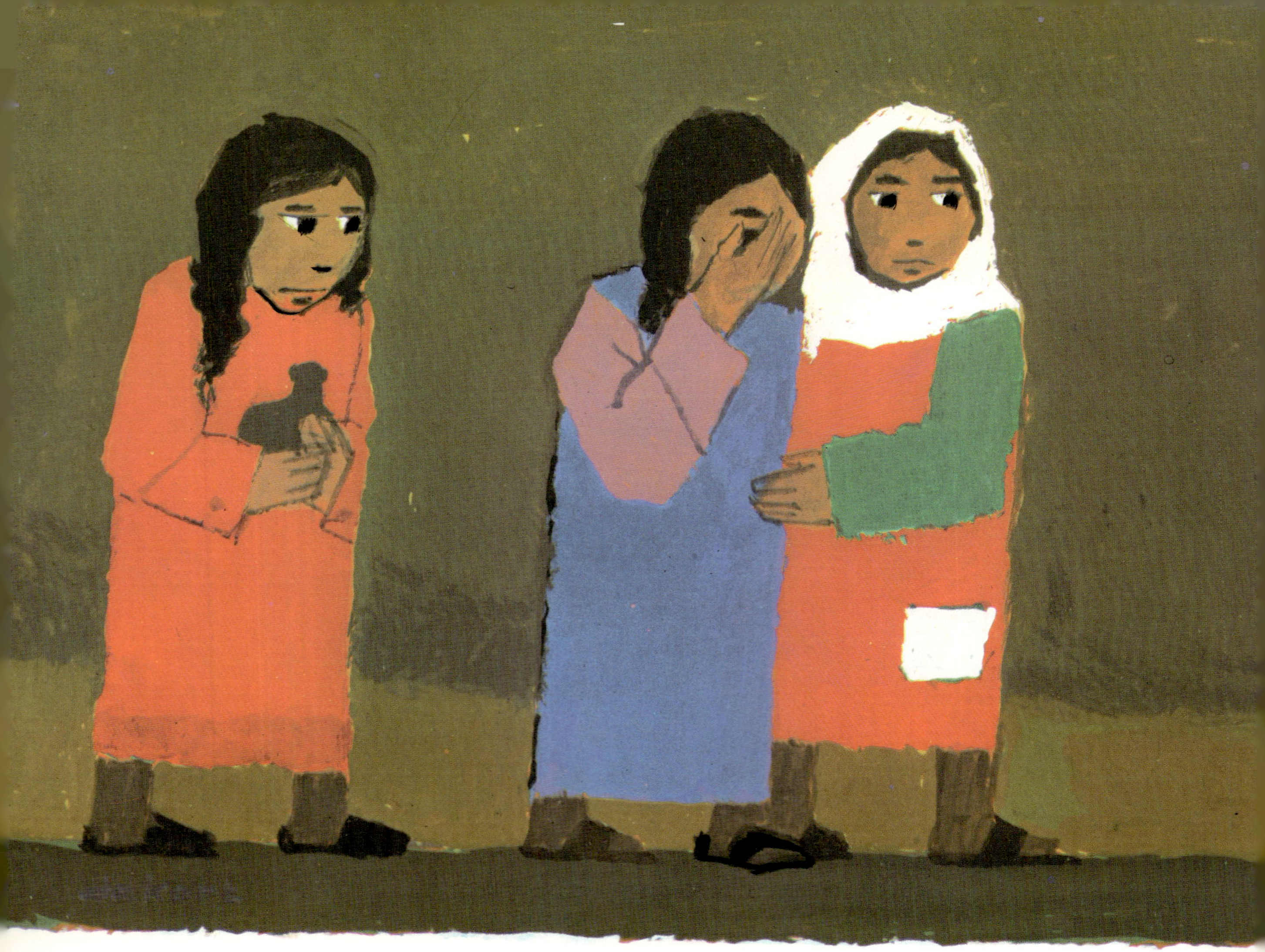

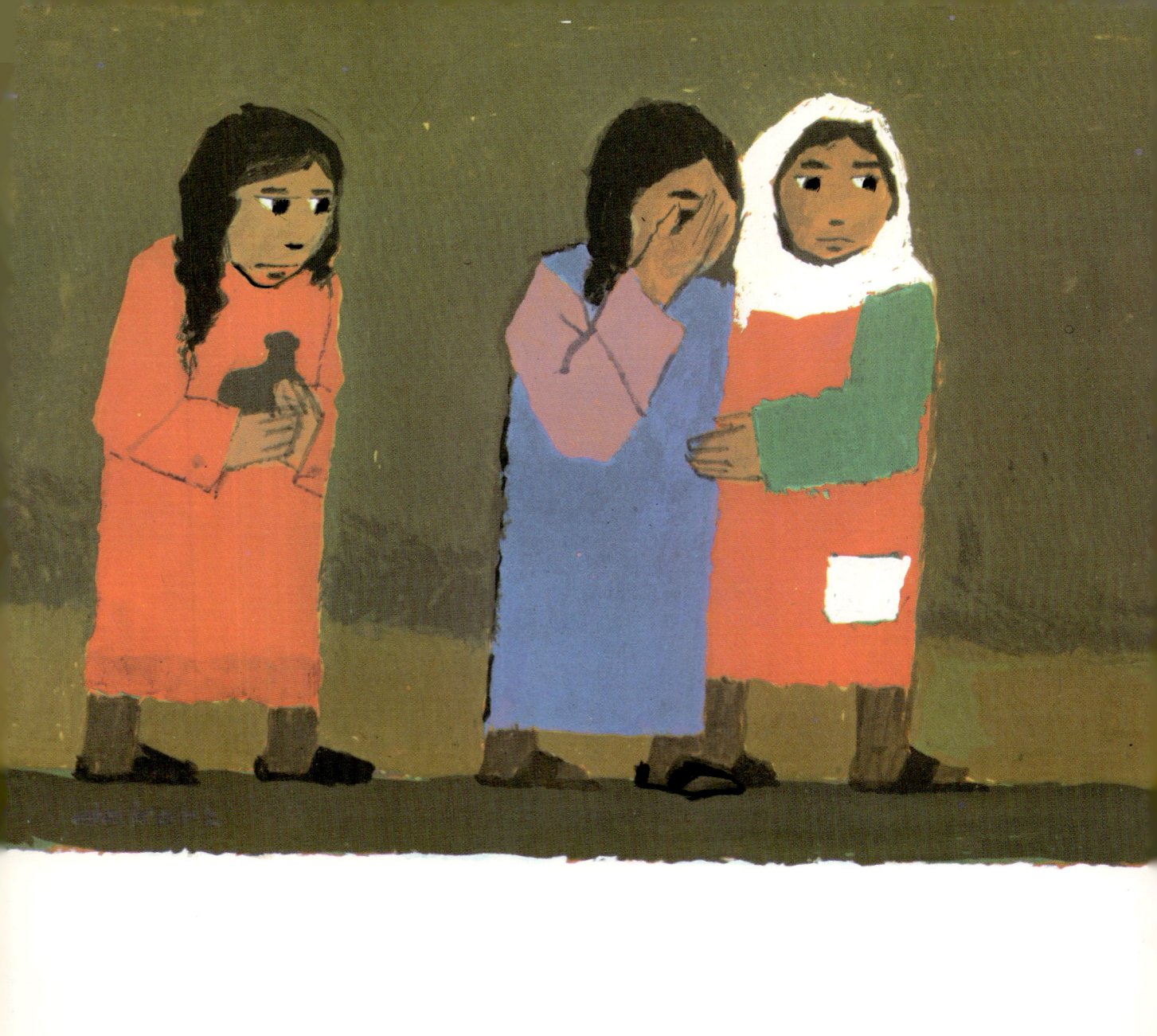

His friends took him down from the cross.
They put him in a cave.

His friends rolled a big stone
in front of the cave.

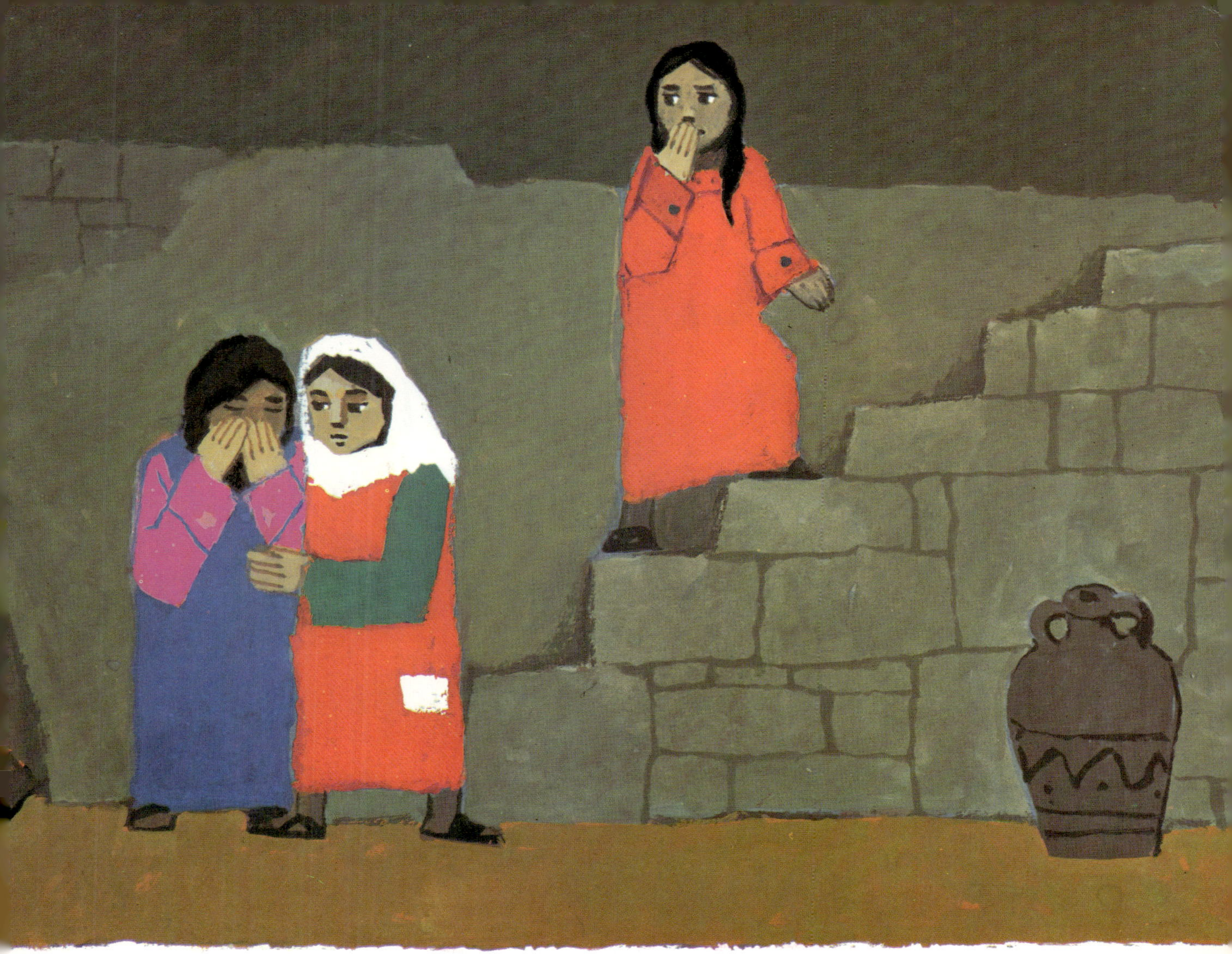

On Sunday morning some women went to the grave but the stone had been moved.
Jesus was not there!

The women saw an angel.
The angel said to them,
"Jesus is alive. Go and tell his friends."

In the evening,
two men were walking to the town of Emmaus.
They talked about Jesus.
They were sad that he had died.

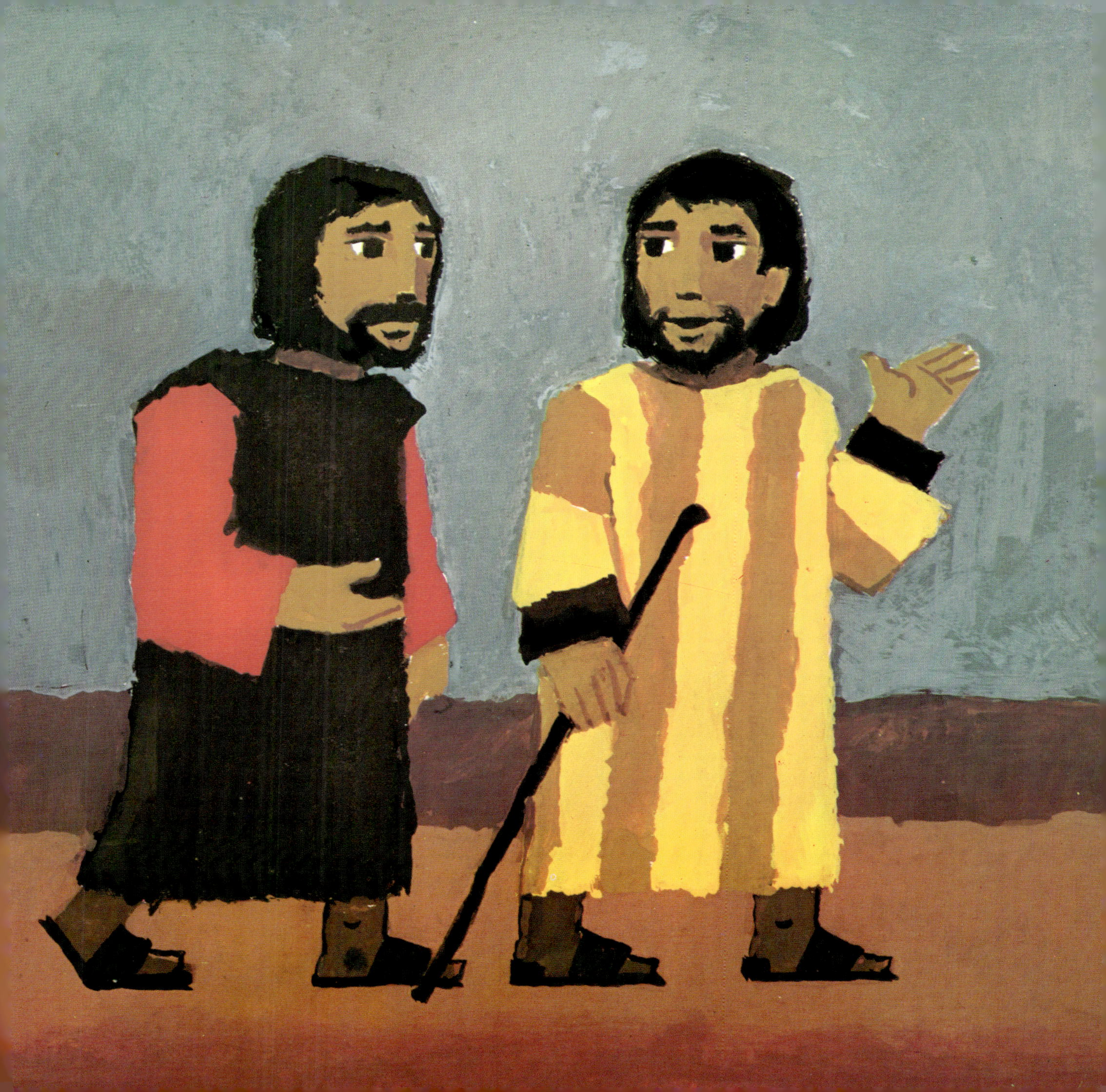

Just then, Jesus came near them.
They did not know who he was.

He told them many things.
He told them why Jesus had to die.

Soon they came to Emmaus.
The men said,
"Come and eat with us."

Jesus went into the house and sat down at the table.
Jesus said thank you to God for the food.
Then the two men knew that it was Jesus.

Suddenly Jesus went away.

The two men ran back to Jerusalem to tell Jesus' friends. "Jesus is alive," they said. "We have seen him!"

As they talked, Jesus came and stood in the room.
His friends were afraid.

Jesus said, "It's me."
Then they were happy. They knew Jesus was alive.